W9-CTF-693

CHRISTMAS

A TREASURY OF HOLIDAY FLORALS AND HELPFUL TIPS

FLORISTS' REVIEW

Publisher: Frances Dudley

Design Director: Talmage McLaurin

Project Editor: Susan Liening

Art Director: Kate Wootton

Production Assistant: Tami Andrews

Photographers: Stephen Smith, Kate Wootton

Floral Design: Talmage McLaurin, AIFD;

Bill Harper, AIFD; Matt Wood, AIFD; Tracy Proctor, AIFD;

David Porterfield, AIFD; Terry Lanker;

Curtis Godwin, AIFD; Phil Marvin; Joe Smith, AIFD

INTRODUCTION

Over the past few years, we have published literally hundreds of photographs of Christmas designs and decorations in *Florists' Review* magazine. And as the library of idea-filled pictures grew larger, we began to think how nice it would be to share the best of them in a holiday book. The result is in your hands.

Including some of our favorite holiday themes, our "Christmas Looks" section includes everything from warm-hearted homespun to classically rich della Robbia. Here you will find a variety of design ideas, all presented within one of six popular holiday themes.

Our "Christmas Ideas" section overflows with special designs, from stately topiaries to wondrous wreaths to glittering candle arrangements, and much more. A great resource for inspired ideas.

To help you identify some must-have holiday products, like pine cones and Christmas greens, "Christmas Elements" is a mini-glossary of care and handling tips that you'll refer to every year.

Our book was carefully edited to provide you with inspiration and ideas. And, in the spirit of *Florists' Review* magazine, this book offers a practical approach to professional floral design.

Frances Dudley
Publisher

Talmage McLaurin, AIFD
Design Director

CHRISTMAS

LOOKS

IDEAS

ELEMENTS

Christmas Looks

Homespun and Antique

Christmas Memories

Christmas is a time for nostalgia. Antique replicas and homespun toys and ornaments bring back memories of a time when Christmas was enchanting and wondrous. Angels, toys, and images of Santa Claus conjure up special childhood memories for all of us. Decorating with antique replicas, like some of the products featured here, is an easy and inexpensive way to recreate those treasured memories year after year for your friends and family.

An elegant yet whimsical wreath (opposite page) hangs on a brick wall over a setting of toys and ornaments reminiscent of yesteryear. Containing luxurious velvet fruits and flowers, an arrangement in a wooden basket adds to the setting's allure. The garland of balls covered with beans, corn, and peas is a novel, natural accessory. Toys include a lovable stuffed teddy bear and a hand-carved, wooden carousel horse tricycle that will enchant nostalgia buffs. Rich-looking wooden trays, a crocheted doily, and pretty corked bottles filled with colorful potpourri complete the "Grandma's parlor" appeal.

An elegant, antique reproduction birdcage (above) is a versatile accessory with old-world sophistication. The wreath of dried hydrangeas combines soft pastels with a pleasing antique feel.

An heirloom doll carriage (left) with a canvas hood and wicker detailing provides a charming way to hold vintage toys or evergreen arrangements. A whimsical, hand-carved Santa and his reindeer look on as they eagerly wait for Christmas Eve to arrive.

Victorian Splendor

This wreath (right) presents a Victorian look updated for today's Christmas. The splendor of velvet fruits and flowers blends beautifully with the luxurious combination of roses, hydrangeas, and golden rye. Both natural and gilded pine cones are nestled in bits of assorted foliage, adding to the wreath's textural interest. Finished with fine ribbons and shiny ornaments, this wreath is a visual feast perfect for ringing in the holidays.

An abundance of antique-like glass baubles (below); velvet-covered, jeweled ornaments; gold doilies reminiscent of the Victorian era; and a rich, gold-edged ribbon provide all the elements for a classically-styled centerpiece. Rich jewel tones, including varying shades of purple, deep burgundies, and reds, with a bright blue ball, result in a Victorian presentation that is modern enough for today's holiday entertaining. Slightly formal, this holiday arrangement is versatile enough for any elegant setting.

The topiary (opposite page) is a soft interpretation of Victorian elegance. A flower lover's favorite, the topiary combines delicate silk blossoms with naturally dried roses, permanent crab apples, lotus pods, and tansy blossoms. The fabric blossoms, resembling old-fashioned millinery flowers, give the arrangement a classic antique look. Emerging from a terra-cotta garden pot, this topiary is garnished with ribbons of coordinating gold-striped organza.

Preserved and fabric flowers can be hot-glued directly onto a topiary form. Mixing both types of flowers adds an old-fashioned look.

Father Christmas

Traditional Christmas elements have firmly rooted themselves as mainstays in seasonal decorations. The timeless appeal and attic-aged appearance of vintage toys and ornaments have a romantic allure. Their beauty provides a sense of history and brings back fond holiday memories.

Laden with toys, this festive Christmas wreath (below) represents the spirit of the season. The combination of maroon and red is subtle, accenting the antique look of this design. Strands of gauzy ribbon and fronds of permanent foliage adorn this classic display of good cheer.

Flanked by red candles topping elegant golden candlesticks, this exquisite centerpiece (above) is perfect for Christmas dinner or other holiday entertaining. Rivers of red ribbon, red-lacquered blossoms, ornaments featuring Father Christmas, and pine cones are nestled in a woven, gold basket. Other elements of this classic centerpiece are gilded grape clusters, preserved juniper, latex ivy, and permanent roses. Intricately-decorated black and red ornaments add a festive touch. The arrangement is striking against a forest green tablecloth.

Father Christmas (right), French ribbon, and a cluster of dried fruits and flowers grace the handle of a stylish holiday basket. The basket is given a natural look by lining it with alternating rows of pine cones, straw flowers, and dried apple slices. The paper cutout of Father Christmas, a mythical figure recognizable to all, is a vintage Christmas image that truly recreates a sense of seasonal nostalgia.

Gingham and Calico

Randomly placed gingham and calico patches cover the cone-shaped tree, wreath, and basket,

while a trio of soft-sculpture snowmen watches over a sheet of freshly baked cookie ornaments.

Remember making cookies using a cookie cutter and playing with soft, patchwork toys? Old-fashioned ornaments and decorations using those familiar themes are part of the homespun Christmas style that appeals to "kids" of all ages.

Touches of red and green fabric in a crazy patchwork design give common objects that nostalgic look of years past. Premade wreaths and "Christmas tree" cones are easy to transform into homespun crafts. Assorted shapes and sizes of festive fabrics are glued directly onto the items.

Permanent strawberries (below), pine cone picks, and fresh evergreens fill the patchwork-covered vase, and the burlap and gingham-covered ornament is ready to be hung on the Christmas tree.

This little button bear (above) is all ready for Christmas, just resting on a bed of fresh greens in his gingham-ruffled basket. Gingham ribbon and permanent strawberries are included in the willow basket. Burlap and gingham ornaments, covered with buttons and big stitches, complete the cozy holiday setting.

Patchwork-covered, stuffed animals and cookie-shaped ornaments are inexpensive crafts that will give holiday decorations a homespun look. Children can help out, adding to the fun. Gingham and calico scraps turn everyday items into country-style crafts that will warm your heart.

Candy Christmas

A riotous mixture of product is combined to create a bright, whimsical delight of a wreath (left) built on a willow base. Holly, berries, kiwi slices, red freesias and poppies, strawberries, and purple alstroemeria dance among the red, white, and celadon ribbons. A pair of jaunty elves adds to the joyous mood.

Wonders from a Christmas kitchen adorn this appetizing wreath (right). To make, combine papier-mâché frosted cookie ornaments, candy canes, and apples. Mix in cross-stitched and gingham ornaments. Season with velvet ribbon, gold ornaments, and other accessories to taste! Place on a door after making.

A plastic apple (above) is dipped in hot pan melt glue to create this mouth-watering faux candy apple. Perfect for a Christmas tree ornament or hostess gift.

This tabletop tree (above) is created from red and white candies and is based in a simple pot sprayed with a glossy red lacquer.

Candy-striped carnations (left) echo the peppermint sticks, making a sweet treat. A few well-placed berried holly branches add just the right highlights.

Glitter and Gold

A simple etching, with an elaborate gold frame, is ringed with a lush garland of eucalyptus. Two silver

candlesticks add height to a row of angels making music amid votive candles and glittering ornaments.

Crystal Clear

Sophistication and sparkle, elegance and refinement. Iridescent and transparent, etched, cut, frosted and iced. The clear fascination of crystal is evident everywhere this yuletide. Evoking the crispness of an icy winter day, crystal gracefully turns from timeless to today and mixes delicately with golds, silvers, and whites.

Natural lichens and mosses (right) sharply contrast with gold ribbons and brass-gilded ornaments in this stately tabletop tree.

A celebration of crystal, gold, and snowy white (below) is presented by this assemblage of a brass cornucopia overflowing with faceted grapes, frosted holly leaves, golden roping, and cut and etched glass baubles. Crystal sparkles even more brightly in the flickering light of pale gold and white candles.

A cluster of crystal grapes (below) and a sheer bow add elegance to this simply wrapped package.

Ribbons and Glitz

Gold adds a richness to holiday decorations; a touch of gold makes everything extraordinary! Christmas is an ideal time to use fabulous gold ribbons. This photograph showcases the versatility of gold ribbon. A pomander of freeze-dried roses, nestled among loops of elegant wired ribbon, makes a striking decoration or Christmas tree ornament. Rich gold cording can be casually coiled to form a gilded bird's nest. When placed atop graceful candlesticks, spheres that are covered with choice ribbons make beautiful custom ornaments or contemporary topiaries. Ribbon roses are especially luxurious when made of wired gold organza. When adorned with a flourish of tasteful ribbon, an everday glass vase can be turned into a decorator piece. Common objects gleam when garnished with gold.

This glittery Christmas design (opposite page) achieves sophistication with a wide variety of products. Metallic gold, silver, and bronze paints can be used to spray ornaments, or use gilded dried materials that are commercially available. In this arrangement, gold lamé and wicker stars immediately attract your attention. A horizontally-placed wheat sheaf is fastened to the basket, and various dried products, including gilded holly leaves, are added in clusters. The arrangement's strong horizontal focus is balanced by the height of the vertical preserved materials, including foxtail grass, lotus pods, and gracefully curled ting-ting. The striking combination of shining metallic ornaments and unusual dried materials gives this trendy holiday arrangement a golden glow.

A twig wreath lavished with rye bundles and fruit in all sizes and shapes is spray painted gold,

creating a glorious gilded wreath. Clusters of crystal grapes scattered around the wreath add to the impact.

Gilded Treasures

Gilded ivy (below) and a mesh bow add sparkle to an arrangement featuring stems of lavender, cones, dried roses, and a nest with a golden egg.

A simple straw wreath (above) is painted gold and accented with gilded rye, curled pheasant feathers, ribbon roses, and berries. Feathers are curled by rubbing their veins against the dull edge of a knife.

Clear vases (above) are turned into candleholders when filled with cranberries and wrapped with cedar. Apple candles, with their flames reflecting on gold ornaments, add a festive touch.

Underwater Gold

Featuring starfish, gilded foliage, and premade, shell-covered ornaments, these nautical designs will bring "sea"sonal riches into the home. This unique tableau (below) creates an underwater feel with its seaweed-like foliage and golden shells and starfish. As holiday decorations, seashells are as unusual as pine cones are traditional. Nautical containers finish the look.

The nautical theme is continued in the twig wreath (opposite page) studded with shell-covered ornaments, sea urchins, and starfish. Evergreens and saxicola, along with an assortment of gilded foliage, are added for effect. Jute rope is sprayed gold and coiled around a burnished pillar candle, and several gilded starfish dangle on pins pushed into the gold taper.

Old World Elegance

During the Middle Ages, adventurous Europeans explored new lands, cultures, and customs. Many of
these travelers brought back luxurious fabrics and incorporated them into their lifestyles. The opulent
designs on these pages combine fruits, florals, and beaded or jeweled ornaments, as well as luxurious
silks, brocades, and velvets. The rich, elaborate arrangements perfectly capture the abundance of the era.

Brocades and Baubles

Nestled among the swirls of gold roping (opposite page) are two types of permanent orchids and a random display of velvet fruit. An ornament, covered in gold and purple brocade, and a stained glass candle reflect the popular, jewel-tone colors often found in medieval designs. Two permanent, gilded artichokes add an exotic touch, as do glittering sun and moon Christmas tree ornaments dangling from loops of gold rope.

An eclectic arrangement (above) features an assortment of one-of-a-kind ornaments. Leaves, seeds, and grains cover spherical ornaments, while others are adorned with faux jewels and gold cording. Other gold accents are added with puffy, fabric stars and a braided cording with tassels. This distinctive arrangement also has an ornate angel ornament tucked in among the greens and a Nordic St. Nick cheerfully waving from the top.

An overflowing collection (below) of elegant, fabric-covered Christmas tree ornaments and permanent botanicals, along with a mystical Venetian carnival figurine, makes this grandiose design enchanting.

Czarist Influence

Like Europe, the former Soviet Union offers the West a rich culture from which dynamic design styles can be drawn. Resembling the skyline of St. Petersburg itself, this opulent collection (below) includes a decorator birdcage, a Byzantine picture frame, and classically styled angels. Intricately detailed filigree ornaments accent the luxurious velvet grapes. For an international Christmas, the jewel-encrusted crosses and embroidered ornaments are the perfect touch.

Holiday Classics

Spilling over with clusters of permanent grapes, this antique brass chalice (below) is filled with ruscus, red sweetheart roses, stock, eucalyptus, and snapdragons. A pair of antique candleholders continue the sweeping lines of the chalice and add a majestic accent, especially when accompanied by additional clusters of richly colored Concord grapes.

Festive fabrics and ribbons (above) are showcased in this elegant tabletop grouping. Damask-covered ornaments and matching wire-edged ribbon combine with a striped brocade tablerunner to create a cordial holiday setting containing an arrangement of permanent dahlias, grasses, and latex holly. A tartan-clad Santa Claus arrives just in time for Christmas with a bag of toys flung over his shoulder. The beautiful tabletop grouping also includes pretty, pillow-shaped sachets crafted from matching velvets and brocades and tied with braided gold cording. A single brass candlestick with a burgundy taper is attractively adorned with dahlias, permanent holly, and ribbon. An elegant brass bowl brimming with colorful potpourri provides a fragrant accent to this attractive Christmastide tableau.

European Elegance

European élan is reflected in the silver vases and candlesticks (opposite page) while a distinct spirit of opulence appears in the florals. Permanent violets, hydrangeas, and regal purple and red peonies are laced together with wired, organza ribbon.

A stately topiary (above) is easily created with tapestry-covered ornaments and a rich, gold-edged ribbon.

An ornate candelabrum (left) is garlanded with parchment poinsettias, burgundy silk roses, berries, and holly.

The look of royal splendor lends lavishness to Christmas decorations. Deep reds, majestic purples, elegant ribbons, and full-bodied arrangements designed with regal grandeur compose the look that fashions this noble, European style.

A golden cherub is the dramatic focus of this opulent wreath of evergreens and vines. Mixed with permanent

flowers, fruits, and berries, gilded mirror Christmas tree ornaments add reflection and dimension.

Gilded Grandeur

Heavily gilded boxes (right), candle-sticks, figurines, and accessories define this ornately elegant look.

The majestic color of gloxinias adds to the arrangement's sumptuous style.

Dried hydrangeas (above) are surrounded by velvet grapes and apples in this unusual holiday arrangement. Winding through the fruit and foliage, a gold-bordered, festively colored ribbon accents the design's predominantly autumn colors. Sprigs of ivy and calycina artfully sprout from the sides of the arrangement. When used as a table centerpiece, the design adds a Gothic, old-world feel to a traditional holiday table.

The beauty of the holiday season can be richly expressed with elegant fabric ribbons (below) in the intense colors of precious gems.

An everyday vase is transformed into a treasure when wrapped with ribbon and enhanced with cording and a multi-ribbon bow, but decorator vases need only be embellished with fine ribbon. And foam balls, when wrapped with ribbon, are transformed into modern ornaments. The splendor of ribbons is as limitless as your imagination.

Woodland Naturals

Forest Findings

A renewed appreciation for nature's bounty leads to a natural celebration of the Christmas season. A distinctive organic look is achieved using nuts, pods, cones, twigs, and other natural products. Gold and silver ribbons provide glittery accents to the woodland items.

A winged elm branch (below) becomes a canopy handle over a moss and twig planter filled with Mother Nature's gifts. The basket is filled to overflowing with lotus pods, pine cones, and preserved cedar. The lone pine-needle nest and scattered golden pine cones add the perfect finishing touches.

A simple arrangement (above) of Christmas greenery combines branches of pine, cedar, and fir punctuated with pine cones and bronze-colored ornaments. Assorted combinations of commercial evergreens are long lasting and perfectly appropriate for holiday arrangements if the containers are kept full of water.

Three conical topiaries (opposite page), resembling little Christmas trees, are trimmed with mosses and cones. A birch shadow box is filled with pine cone rosettes, preserved moss, cedar, cinnamon, and lotus pods, while pine cones, lotus pods, and preserved cedar fill a twig and moss planter. Premade trees, generously covered with pine cones, snuggle in the grouping along with a wooden, green-washed container of pine cones and pods. Individual pieces of green dinnerware, a rustic twig basket, and wooden candlesticks topped by basil green candles accent the entire collection of woodland Christmas décor.

A collection of pine cones, dried pods, and turkey quills creates this rustic tree. Its base is covered with jute

rope, and the dried products are glued on and between coils of rope. A wooden tub completes the design.

Feathered Friends

The vertical gathering of pine cones (right), highlighted with German statice, French ribbon, curly willow, and slightly curved pheasant feathers, creates a look of seasonal sophistication. The moss-filled bird's nest is a perfect accessory, adding a nice contrast to this otherwise dark, woodsy gathering. Note how the loops of the bow are repeated in the looping branches of curly willow.

Superbly crafted feather ornaments (below) in warm earth tones are accented with burled wood hat boxes, pomegranates, taffeta sachets, and pheasant pelts to create an elegant buffet or mantel grouping.

Christmas Preserves

Woodland naturals lend rustic elegance to the holiday season with preserved foliages that last indefinitely yet have the feel and fragrance of fresh. Often fashioned of pliable, preserved greens incorporated with dried and permanent materials, festive woodland natural creations provide the beauty of the natural outdoors for extended indoor enjoyment during the holiday season.

An abundance of naturally dried lemons (opposite page), pomegranates, and pinion pine cones are perched among branches of preserved juniper. Resting atop red dogwood branches, the arrangement becomes a beautiful holiday topiary in a simple wooden container.

Christmas cheer is wrapped up in a wreath (above) featuring a wondrous array of preserved products glued onto a twig form. A nesting partridge makes its home among preserved holly, fern, juniper, and boxwood; acorns and mushroom-covered ornaments add charm. The candleholder is fashioned from a peel of birch bark tied with pepperberries and ribbon.

An abundance of red dogwood branches (below) shoot upward from a rectangular planter that is generously embellished with dried lemons, pomegranates, preserved juniper, pine cones, and boxwood. The birdhouse, roofed with red dogwood twigs, matches the bundle of twigs tied up with a wire ribbon bow. Adornments include cream and mulberry beeswax candles set "just so" in their elegant brass candleholders; carved, wooden angels; and two golden mesh boxes filled with fragrant holiday potpourri.

Prairie Passage

A column of barley surrounded by rye (left) is striking in a birch bark planter ringed by pine cones, pods, canella berries, and boxwood.

Spice up naturals with brass candlesticks and beeswax candles (below); a brass bowl filled with pomegranates; and a unique wreath filled with acorns, pencil cattails, pheasant feathers, and a variety of striking pods.

An unusual combination of dried pods (opposite page), pheasant feathers, and cattails are combined to form the rustic Christmas tree. This look has seasonal appeal but is created with products available year-round.

Natural Gold

Natural materials, rough-hewn and handcrafted, are key elements in this look (opposite page). Washed with gold, these items retain their natural appearances and gain a touch of elegance. A windswept design of preserved cedar, berried

branches, eucalyptus seed pods, cones, and balls resembles a thicket sheltering a gilded birdhouse. The conical topiary in a gold clay pot incorporates the same principle of using natural materials highlighted with gold. The natural beeswax candles are the perfect accessory to complete the look.

The Pacific Northwest provides the inspiration (above) for this soothing mixture of deciduous branches, evergreens, and lichens. Native mosses, pine cones, and mushrooms add variety. A wonderful accompaniment is the bronze deer, looking as though it could spring out of its concealing thicket at any moment.

A branch basket (left) is given the gold treatment with a light coat of paint. The nest's look is natural yet dressed for Christmas.

This stylish arrangement (below) is beautiful because of its simplicity. Exciting texture is achieved with vibrant hedge apples.

The Look of Lodge

A fisherman's creel is the center of a rustic potpourri of trout candlesticks, a needlepoint picture frame, a Santa gone "au naturel," acorns, pine cones, and a faux rabbit pelt. A woven wreath, garnished with a spray of permanent berries and Christmas-colored ribbons, is a festive accessory for decorating.

A key element of this successful tabletop grouping is the color coordination and the combination of interesting textures. Splashes of reds and deep greens are striking against straw colors. The honeycomb candles, jute wreath, and needlepoint frame add various textures to this rustic setting.

Nature's Bounty

Homespun and handcrafted, rustic and comfortable. Natural and outdoorsy, heart-warming and homey. The lodge look features masculine presentations such as Native American designs in warm, earthy tones; gone fishin' ornaments; and arrangements that tie in with the woodland natural look.

A natural panorama is presented (below) by grass-covered and faux wooden orbs nestled among evergreens, oregonia, eucalyptus, winterberry, pheasant feathers, hydrangeas, and miniature crimson carnations. Chipmunk twins and a lone pine cone extend the look, which is based in a rough-hewn, woodland textured container.

The companion centerpiece (above) is built on a foam cage set atop a solid birch "stump." The mixture of flowers is similar to the variety used in the larger design, but a lotus pod and a crimson taper are added for extra color and textural variety.

A bark-covered birdhouse (upper left) is given holiday flair with a few bits of evergreen, gilded leaves, and preserved red roses.

Crisp Christmas Colors

Three kinds of bright red berries—holly, cotoneaster, and bush honeysuckle—play a festive Christmas tune with limes, red roses, freesias, and ivy (right). A beeswax candle in a galvanized steel candleholder is adorned by a satin ribbon bedecked with Christmas colors. Vivid red cranberries, in a gilded terra-cotta tray, and an ornament covered with mushroom slices, round out the woodsy, cozy grouping. The bark basket adds rich brown hues that complement the design's crisp and bold Christmas colors. This arrangement is sure to be an annual holiday favorite.

A lone lure (above) adds charm to this permanent arrangement of berry clusters, vines, pine cones, and natural, grass-covered spheres. The bark container gives the design a masculine look.

Elements of Lodge

This is the perfect package for every man who loves to fish. A box wrapped simply in brown paper (center) sports a festive, new look with the addition of a bright plaid bow; permanent leaves and acorns; and a fun, painted-metal fish. The message is clear: Gone fishin'!

Besides the rustic look typical of woodland natural arrangements and the outdoorsy look associated with fish, the lodge presentation gains a masculine, earthy feel from Native American icons, symbols, and designs.

The lodge evergreen wreath (right) is decorated with spherical ornaments covered with mushrooms, cranberries, clusters of grapes, pine cones, and curled pheasant feathers. Interspersed among the natural products are Native American elements including tiny dream weavers, a miniature canoe, and an intricately-detailed, beaded leather moccasin.

Earth-centered in look and texture, lodge and woodland natural designs pay respect to the environment, bringing elements of nature indoors for long-lasting enjoyment. Woodland natural designs differ slightly from lodge designs in that they often incorporate birds and birds' nests as well as natural materials. Lodge arrangements tend to feature more masculine artifacts that bring the elements of earth, sky, and water to mind. Both are popular holiday themes.

Della Robbia

The della Robbia tradition of combining fruit and flowers is depicted in this French-country-inspired arrangement (right). Leaving the copper trim exposed, galvanized steel containers are painted black and adorned to create a fruit-print motif. The apple in the center of the taller arrangement has been color treated with a glossy wood-toned paint.

Single pieces of permanent fruit (below) are sprayed with adhesive and covered with spices such as whole black peppercorns, oregano, parsley, and paprika.

From Elegance to Country Charm

Since the 15th century and the days of Florentine sculptor Luca della Robbia, lavish fruit and flower fantasies have been part of the holidays. The artist's name has become synonymous with the technique of covering terra-cotta botanical garlands with brightly colored enamel glazes. The sculptured garlands were, in turn, used to frame molded depictions of religious scenes. Designs that incorporate the della Robbia look can include a range of styles—from old-world baroque to French country. The opulent combination of fruit and flowers in the della Robbia tradition lends elegance to today's Christmas decorating.

A traditional bellpull (above) is festooned with a delightful lacing of grape clusters, apples, pears, and peaches. To create the bellpull, wrap two or more permanent berry branches together to form a base. Twist one end of the base into a loop to create a hanger. Hot-glue artificial fruit, flowers, and ribbon to the base, and finish off with a tailored bow at the top.

Visit this charming "country store" table display (right) fashioned of soft drink crates. The della Robbia-garnished basket and tiny terra-cotta pots filled with fruit topiaries have been sprayed gold. To create the simple topiaries, fruit-laden branches can be inserted directly into foam-filled pots, or single pieces of fruit can be pierced and glued onto twigs.

50 Della Robbia

Della Robbia
Table Treatments

A wreath of royal, jewel-tone colors (opposite page), ranging from raspberry to plum, is a pleasure to behold. Ivy, cedar, echinops, Concord grapes, and purple plums are highlighted by spherical and tapered candles, all based in an everyday foam form.

Della Robbia candleholders (above) give Christmas parties an exciting look. Wooden candle extenders, oranges, lemons, pears,

and two different kinds of apples are used to create this unique presentation. The pieces of fruit are pierced and placed on the extenders with fresh yarrow, salal leaves, and variegated pittosporum dotted in for framing. Both pots and candle extenders are spray-painted gold for Christmas sparkle.

Snapdragons, ivy, and cedar (left) overflow from a cluster of pomegranates, sliced limes, and candles, all collected in a blue, patina-finished urn. Christmas colors are reflected in the dark green and red hues.

52 Della Robbia

Home and Hearth

This mantel (opposite page) is a classic setting for showcasing the lush della Robbia style. The traditional elegance of della Robbia is perfect for a beautiful Christmas presentation. Bountiful fruits, ivy, ornaments, and candles, along with a generous della Robbia wreath, add sophisticated accents.

A basket, literally overflowing with dried and permanent materials (below), makes an early-autumn-through-winter statement. Bark-toned cabbage roses and moss mix with dried sunflowers, celosia, and highly fragrant sweet Annie. Pumpkins, gourds, pomegranates, and feathers complete the bountiful harvest look that adds drama to any entry.

Ruby-red pomegranates (above) nestle among a woodsy assemblage of pine cones, acorns, berries, and preserved greens. A gold-edged, citron and burgundy ribbon adds color and elegance.

A freestanding twig sphere (below), covered with natural grasses, is perfect for a small space and represents an earthy twist to the traditional della Robbia style.

Flickering Candles

The twinkling flame of a candle adds life to any arrangement. Relatively inexpensive, candles provide warmth and sophistication. But, a candle is not meant to sit silently in the middle of a design. It should be alight, sparking the celebration and eliciting cheer and good will.

Elegant red and cranberry candles (below) tower above a stunning mix of foliage. Fir, oregonia, and heather, along with pine cone rosettes and bright green apples, create holiday harmony. Gold-painted montbretia and gourds add brilliance to a complementary color combination.

Fruit, flowers, and candles combine to give holiday decorations a warm, soothing glow. To create this tabletop wreath (right), glue tiny clay pots to the edge of an inverted clay saucer. Secure the candles in the pots with low temperature glue or florist clay. Add a foam-filled, plastic saucer to the center for the florals.

A round, red candle (below) is ringed by green amaranthus, cedar, and montbretia pods.

Roses echo the red, and fragrant lemon slices fill out the form and add a colorful contrast.

This design (below) combines an extravagant and colorful blend of traditional Christmas colors. Unusual candles, which appear to have a bark-like texture, are placed amid green ivy and fir, which accent the variety of reds. All of the components except the ivy will dry in place.

A fruited festoon is filled with permanent pomegranates, grapes, apples, and peaches. The tree-shaped form, placed atop a brass candlestick appears to be an epergne, spirally encrusted with the same fruits. The space between is filled with moss to allow for an uncluttered line. Gold cording and tall taper candles in classic brass candlesticks add an elegant holiday feeling.

Gold Ribbon Bounty

This combination of papier-mâché fruits and berries (right), resplendent with vibrant persimmon and dark bittersweet, is perfect for a formal setting. The look is topped off with bright splashes of gold cording and ripples of golden ribbon.

Colorful brocade (below) is combined with assorted permanent berries and pomegranates in this opulent design. Hatboxes wrapped in gold and a small birdcage add a decorator accent.

Citrus and Spice

Although the crisp colors of citrus fruits are not traditional Christmas hues, they provide a refreshing alternative to standard red and green. This contemporary holiday presentation features classic urns filled with cone-shaped topiaries of artificial lemons and magnolia foliage. A single candle in the center of the coordinating wreath illuminates the setting. Magnolia foliage swags complete this clean Christmas presentation.

Oranges and Spices

Fragrances are part of the heartwarming memories associated with the holidays of one's lifetime. Whether the Christmas air was filled with the smells of Grandma's sage stuffing or spicy pomander balls, redolent aromas have evoked Christmas memories since colonial Williamsburg, when fruits were widely used in decorations. Today, the colors and scents of oranges, lemons, and limes add a fresh twist to traditional Christmas arrangements and bring back fond remembrances of Christmases past. And, tabletop decorations of fruits and flowers add warmth to family gatherings.

Made of citrus fruits and spices, pomander balls (above left) are a popular gift item that add a welcoming aroma to a holiday home. From exotic, star-shaped anise to the traditional standbys of cinnamon and cloves, spices please the eye and perfume the air. Creating clove-studded orange pomander balls is a happy tradition for many. Along with a spicy citrus pomander, cinnamon sticks bundled with matching gold cording can be used to create a fragrant decoration ideal for an informal table or as a Christmas tree ornament.

A steel container (below) sprouts a veritable garden of spices, sprigs of berried juniper, and freeze-dried lemon slices. Nutmeg, rose hips, anise, cinnamon, and bay leaves are all used in custom-made potpourri that accompanies a citrus-colored candle.

Fresh and unique, arrangements of festive fruits, spices, and flowers will bring a bright new look to your holiday bouquets and announce to all: Let the Christmas season begin!

Spiced Fruit

A delightful basket (center) arrives for the holidays. Three perfect, paprika-covered peaches snuggle in the corner of the moss basket, which has been coated with spray adhesive to retain sprinklings of spices, including parsley and oregano. Holly, sprays of canella berries, and a gold-trimmed ribbon add seasonal flourishes. A perfect gift idea for your favorite cook or herb gardener, the spice basket can also hold a few small canisters of individual spices tucked in among the greens. This spice basket is practical and pretty!

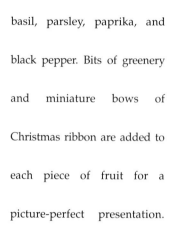

Inexpensive plastic apples, lemons, and oranges (below) are coated with spray adhesive and sprinkled with various herbs, including oregano, basil, parsley, paprika, and black pepper. Bits of greenery and miniature bows of Christmas ribbon are added to each piece of fruit for a picture-perfect presentation. The weathered, wooden crate adds a rustic touch that nicely complements the spices and adds an antique touch to any kitchen. Crate sections are filled with cut Styrofoam® blocks, sprayed with adhesive, and sprinkled with herbs.

OREGANO

PAPRIKA

BASIL

BLACK PEPPER

PARSLEY

Pears and Citrus

Providing a unique twist on the standard urn, this collapsible wooden stand (below) supports a weighty cluster of fresh citrus accessories. The stands are topped with lemons, limes, oranges, shiny holiday baubles, and remarkably realistic pear candles. Floral foam, either alone or in a container, can be perched in the top of the stand. Wooden picks are inserted into the fruit, then inserted into the foam. Italian ruscus adds a light touch. The brightly colored fruits, foliage, and baubles combine to make these candleholders festive "tabletoppers" that will add pizzazz to any holiday party.

Columnar candleholders consisting of cut or whole lemons and oranges provide color and strong geometric appeal as a festive table-top centerpiece. Citrus fruits (above) are stacked and skewered on a hyacinth stake or on a thin wooden dowel (shish kebab style!), with a bright red beeswax candle adding holiday panache. Snippets of Italian ruscus leaves are tucked in between the skewered columns of fruit and the ends of the candles. Shiny ball ornaments adorned with additional leaves reflect the flame and add to the party's glow.

Cranberry Days

A sphere of pavéd cranberries makes a stunning statement for holiday entertaining. The ruby-red color is

repeated in the flowers, creating a dramatic, elevated centerpiece. The cranberries are attached to a Styrofoam®

ball with wooden toothpicks. The rich hues of cranberries provide a sharp contrast to the dark green foliage.

Cranberries, one of the few native American fruits, lend themselves well to bright, beautiful arrangements.

Mixed Fruit Tabletop Garnishes

Combining a palette of several varieties of fruits in unexpected juxtapositions delights the eye, brightens the atmosphere, and entices the palates of partygoers. An inexpensive, glass vase (below) holds a rainbow of fruits in fresh water that must be changed daily. Exotic Oriental lilies, sprigs of cedar, and glitzy ornaments can be arranged directly in the vase or they can be placed in a foam-filled cage set atop the vase's opening. Perfect for a special holiday party!

Wine glasses filled with cranberries (above) hold a delightful froth of ruscus and dendrobium orchids, topped with a novel faux apple candle. The foliage and flowers are placed in water tubes hidden by the cranberries.

A copper tray (below) holds an aperitif of pomegranate halves, a sliced lime, sprigs of ivy, bits of evergreen, and a single burgundy candle.

Elegant and Aromatic

A classic bronze urn (opposite page) is enlivened with the addition of loosely arranged branches of cedar and fir. Oranges and handmade pomanders heighten the fragrant sensations, add textural contrasts and play with the colors in the painting. A hand-wired garland of incense cedar serpentines around the table top. Matching candlesticks hold elegant tall candles carefully coordinated to the wall color. This simple but elegant presentation enhances the artwork. In the coordinating centerpiece (center), fresh holiday evergreens, dried fruit slices, pomander balls, and permanent grape clusters complete the arrangement. Glittery gold leaves and bunches of cinnamon sticks wrapped in gold cord add sparkle. Dried fruit slices are readily available from many sources and are an inexpensive, long-lasting way to add bright colors to your favorite holiday arrangements.

Arrangements composed of citrus fruits and fragrant evergreen branches add elegance and sophistication to any room's décor with a look that emphasizes traditional Christmas greenery. Many types of greens, such as noble fir and western red cedar, can last through the holiday season with minimal care. When purchasing greens, select those with firm branches and green needles. Beware of foliage that are fading, turning brown or yellow, or shedding needles.

Christmas greens are often mistakenly assumed to be hardy. However, like other freshly cut products, evergreens need appropriate care and handling in order to prolong freshness. Some evergreens, like balsam and silver fir, can be used outdoors in wreaths and door decorations since they are hardy enough to withstand freezing temperatures. Other greens, like holly and boxwood, are better suited for indoor use.

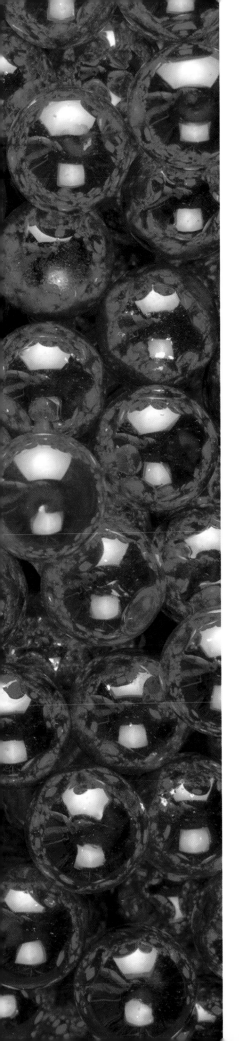

Christmas Ideas

Wreaths and Swags

This unusual swag features crisscrossed sheaves of rye decorated with permanent, pale pink roses, stems of dried lavender, hydrangeas, and two permanent artichokes. Miniature birds' nests with tiny eggs accent both the swag and matching centerpiece. A beautiful birdcage completes the setting.

A twig wreath (above) is adorned with majestic ball ornaments sponged with purple, gold, and red paint. The wreath (below) overflows with permanent magnolia foliage and blossoms. Artichoke-shaped configurations of magnolia leaves rest on pure white petals, filling bronze sconces.

Spherical forms dominate this well-rounded wreath (above). Pretty permanent pomegranates, resembling colorful ornaments, harmonize with berries, grapes, and seeds of every kind. Preserved berried juniper joins the other materials, with the surprise of royal blue organza ribbon adding excitement to this bountiful design. The use of pine cones, pomegranates, permanent rosebuds, and heavy swirls of color-saturated ribbon gives this wreath (below) a rich feel. The blues, pinks, and peaches add softly hued floral romance.

Warm-toned and deeply textured, this wreath (above) can span the holiday season from October through December. The tapestry ribbon adds sophistication.

A nesting partridge (above) finds a happy home among clusters of blue and green grapes, permanent lemon halves, forest green pomegranates, pine cones, and mushroom-covered ball ornaments. Crystal grapes add sparkle throughout the design, which features an inexpensive vinyl wreath as its base. A simple collection of fruit garnishing a fan-shaped sheaf of wheat (right) creates a harvest-inspired door hanging that welcomes the holiday season. The colorful decoration is perfect for a kitchen.

This holiday classic will be hung "on the first day of Christmas." Leafy branches of splendid permanent pears wind through the evergreen wreath. Simple but styled with elegance, this is the perfect gift for a "true love."

This grapevine wreath combines pretty autumn colors displayed in pomegranates, pine cones, and orange slices. As a decoration that heralds the coming of winter, the wreath brings the magnificence of nature indoors.

This wreath, made of berries, seeds, grapes, and dried orange slices, provides a faux feeding refuge for birds. The addition of pine cones, tiny clay pots, and a nest for a feathered friend further enriches the outdoor design.

This exotic wreath evokes the charm of the South with its assortment of magnolia leaves, permanent magnolia blossoms, pine cones, and dried orange slices. Two artificial pineapples add a welcoming touch.

Inspired by the Amish, this charming wreath (above) has a simple, homespun feel that is also found in the quaint child's rocker and the painted boxes. The wreath is decorated with plenty of hand-painted, wooden Christmas tree ornaments. Pine cones and clusters of permanent red berries are mixed in, adding a colorful seasonal accent. In a festive swirl of pine cones, holly, and Christmas-colored tartan ribbon, this twig wreath (left) perfectly captures the joyful spirit of Christmas. Preserved wintergreens are threaded throughout the wreath, adding to its woodland natural look.

This mossy wreath (right) is adorned with ivy, holly, and pomegranates. The moss-covered bow adds an unusual accent. A basket similarly covered in moss and decorated with pomegranates and holly makes a novel candleholder for red and burgundy candles. The swag (below) gives plenty of zip to the Christmas season with its assortment of hot chili peppers. Miniature birds' nests are quaint accents to the sheaves of wheat and the permanent fruits and flowers that compose the design. Perfect for adding style to a country kitchen.

Cranberry red, apple green, and grape purple ribbons (above) meander gracefully through a fanciful fruited wreath, adding just the right stylish accent. The assorted fruit, foliage, and berries are permanent.

A permanent Asian pine wreath (below) serves as the base for this elaborate design. A garland of gold-edged, velvet poinsettias is intertwined and cascades downward. Coordinating ribbon follows the movement of the poinsettias. Permanent fruits and birds' nests provide lots of textural contrast.

Incorporating florals with architectural details, this seasonal doorpiece (above) depicts the splendor and majesty of Christmas with the green and red metallic hound's-tooth ribbon. The leaves of the pre-made garland of permanent materials are made with a powdered finish for a lighter green color. Sprigs of berries and miniature apples add crisp Christmas red.

This fragrant premade wreath (right), formed with clusters of dried herbs, is embellished with metallic gold leaves and a crushed velvet ribbon for a distinctive holiday flair. The clusters of herbs in this seasoned wreath include sage, oregano, lemon mint, and lavender. A chef's special!

A natural twig wreath (below), made over for the season with frosty silver spray paint, is enhanced with a simple linear design of permanent magnolias, roses, and raspberries. The stunning images on the ribbon are worthy of the Sistine Chapel and provide an accent that is simply perfect. A wintery, wonderful wreath to behold.

A swirled twig wreath (above) serves as a base onto which all the materials were glued to create this design. The regal colors of gold and purple were selected to create the theme: gold permanent magnolia and oak leaves, pomegranates, acorns, crackle-finish pears, and purple sinuata statice, which will permanently dry in place. Broadening the dramatic color scheme slightly are multicolored, glass ball ornaments, and a gold-patterned velvet ribbon. This stunning wreath will welcome friends and family.

An eclectic assortment of glorious metallized materials (left), from matte to shiny, create a sumptuous wreath with elegant, yet natural, spirit. Copper leaves, silver gourds, and gold ornaments, accented with pine cones and clumps of moss, cause an exciting textural interplay. Dried eucalyptus leaves impart a fresh fragrance to this permanent design.

Topiaries

Topiary is the art of shaping plants into living sculptures. Although topiaries are traditionally thought of as elaborate, outdoor hedge sculptures, often in the shapes of animals, tabletop topiaries are a twist on the conventional form. Miniature topiaries can be fashioned from plants or from cut flowers, foliage, dried materials, and ribbons.

Topiaries can include unusual elements, such as vegetables, as well as more traditional cut or dried flowers. This novel topiary (above) is made of broccoli florets, roses, and carnations. The broccoli florets are inserted into a premade, conical topiary form with toothpicks. This topiary displays Christmas red and green in a special presentation.

Poplar-shaped pillars (above) are created
by binding incense cedar branches with wire.
The forms rest in beds of moss and pine cones.

Perfect for a
Christmas party, this
elegant, egg-shaped
topiary (right) is created
by covering a piece of wet
floral foam with chicken
wire and inserting fresh
cranberries skewered on
toothpicks. Fresh roses are
then added. For a longer-lasting
topiary, freeze-dried roses
and permanent berries
can be substituted.

Dried fruit slices (left), teasels, pine
cones, and coxcomb cover this conical
topiary. The stems of the dried flowers
are inserted directly into the foam form.
Orange slices are hot-glued into the
form. Colors and groups of dried flowers
are clustered closely together to avoid a
"spotty" effect. An assorted collection of
spice-covered and leaf-covered cones
and orbs repeat the geometric shapes
featured in the topiary. Perfect for
decorating, this topiary is a scaled-down
version of a full-size Christmas tree.

An espalier is a trellis or a frame upon which tree branches are trained to grow. In this contemporary version of the traditional espalier (above), simple sticks of bamboo are wrapped together with raffia to form a lattice-work wall. Permanent pears are attached to the espalier with wire. A rich assortment of permanent and dried florals overflow the wooden window box, with fresh evergreens added for fragrance. Reminiscent of the "Twelve Days of Christmas," partridges flock beneath the permanent pears rather than beneath an old-fashioned pear tree. This pear tree topiary (left) is composed of permanent pears, pear blossoms, and foliage. The base of the topiary is a burlap sack gathered around the trunk and tied with a thin pear branch. The branch is decorated with additional pears and foliage, and its ends are twisted for a natural-looking botanical effect.

This Christmas topiary (left) is resplendent with gold metallic ribbons, red parchment roses, raspberries, and holly. The dried products are inserted into a piece of dry foam hot-glued to the top of the sturdy branch stem. Hydrangeas and a bronzed jingle bell fill the top of the terra-cotta pot.

Holly and ivy are aptly paired in the classic Christmas carol and in this pretty topiary (right). A grouping of smaller birch branches form the stem. Oregonia and bright red ilix berries are added to the topiary, creating a delightful holiday decoration.

This elegant, papier-mâché planter (left) holds a small topiary tree that features an extra wide birch trunk. The sphere of the topiary is composed of grape clusters, bunches of acorns, and wax-coated ivy leaves.

This updated twist on the traditional topiary (below) features stemmed ornaments and silk leaves rather than fresh materials. Clusters of balls are wired together and bound to the top of the stem. The pot was originally covered with ivy leaves that dried in place. A light coat of gold paint gives it a two-toned look. Gold and white ribbon adds the Midas touch.

This topiary (above) makes last minute Christmas entertaining a snap. By combining fresh evergreens with silk flowers and berries, these decorations can be made days in advance of a party. Shiny permanent pomegranates and frosted pine cones are used to elongate this topiary, which can be placed in two's or three's down the length of a long dining table. The crimped gold ribbon is wired directly to the topiary's base, a decorative basket. Table settings in gilded splendor welcome an evening of fine holiday dining.

Two stems of fresh amaryllis (above) are tied together with raffia. The spray-painted pears and terra-cotta pot add shine and elegance.

Christmas colors embellish this festive topiary (above) that is perfect as a tabletop display. Tiny apples are inserted into a premade topiary form, and bright plaid ribbons add a finishing touch. These miniature topiaries and candlesticks (left) form an elegant grouping that serves as a classic centerpiece for Christmas dinner. The premade topiaries are gracefully tied together with a red berry garland. Red bows, edged in gold, add attractive, colorful accents to the setting.

Pussy willows and linear foliage camouflage a cylinder vase that rests on a block of floral foam inside the gilded flower pot. Thin gold wire decoratively binds the branches to the vase. A strikingly contemporary design can be simply created with any flower variety. The ordinary shadow box becomes an imaginative, year-round decoration with bits of nature that can be changed with the seasons. One ornament gives it a Christmas flavor.

Fragrant eucalyptus leaves (below) are artfully pinned to a plastic foam cone in a fish-scale pattern to create a contemporary yet natural seasonal accessory. Red roses are an ideal accompaniment.

A "fence" of dried rose stems (above) conceals a trio of cylinder vases in the center in which the fresh roses, kalanchoe blossoms, and heather are arranged. Fading roses can be replaced to maintain the hedge.

With a papier-mâché-covered balloon as a base (right), galax leaves are glued on to create a natural, modern form. An occasional metallic leaf adds a touch of holiday glamour.

Ornaments

Ornaments accessorize fresh flowers (above) in a novel way. Glass teardrop ornaments are suspended like a tassel from an arrangement featuring agapanthus emerging from a base of Marco Polo heather, evergreens, and hydrangeas. A red votive candle (right) is surrounded by stars and teardrop ornaments placed on wood picks and inserted into the foam base. A dynamic variety of colors and textures characterizes these stunning arrangements.

This stylized seasonal welcome (near right) offers an alternative to the traditional wreath. The impressive ornament hangs from a red velvet ribbon entwined with natural vines. The effect of a marbelized bunch of grapes (far right) is formed by wiring clusters of painted ornaments together and hot-gluing them to luxurious loops of gold cording. An elegant red bow tops it off.

The ornaments on this page were created by dipping ball ornaments into buckets of room-temperature water immediately after the surface of the water was sprayed with red paint. The process was repeated with purple and gold paints. The ornaments were then blotted with a sponge. A plastic ornament (left) is broken and filled with pink minature dried roses. A large, marbelized ornament nestles among permanent violets and dried hydrangeas. Fresh flowers are beautiful accents for these colorful ornaments as well.

A dried pear and an apple are covered with nuts to create these charming decorations that can serve as Christmas tree ornaments or, as shown, in terra-cotta pots as tabletop conversation pieces. Group several for impact.

Complemented by a rich collection of dried materials, these gilded cherubs alight upon a gold-leafed pot. To create, spray gold paint onto the surface of a pan of water. Dip and rotate the pot; the paint will adhere randomly.

Elegant in its simplicity, this design features an apple covered with glitter set atop a gold-leafed pot and enhanced with a few nuts, berries, and a length of gold cording. Perfect as a place setting favor or hostess gift.

Homey holiday handicrafts are brought to mind with a patchwork ornament and other homespun accessories, all embellished with novel button placements and a bundle of red grain. Stitched hearts add a touch of whimsy.

An ornament covered with gold cording and faux jewels gives a sense of majesty to this simple design accented with green canella berries, velvet leaves, preserved cedar, and a simple bow tied of gold mesh ribbon.

A golden, sleeping cherub adds charm to this clay pot filled with fresh red roses and snippets of berried juniper. The roses and evergreens are inserted into a base of floral foam while the angel is wired in among the red roses.

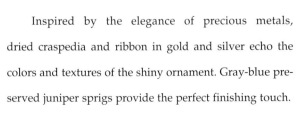

Inspired by the elegance of precious metals, dried craspedia and ribbon in gold and silver echo the colors and textures of the shiny ornament. Gray-blue preserved juniper sprigs provide the perfect finishing touch.

A great Christmas accent for the kitchen or breakfast nook, this aged pot full of apples and berries has holiday appeal. A festive sparkle is added with miniature glass ornaments and the metallic threads in the plaid ribbon.

This contemporary Christmas tree is made of foam-centered board painted a shiny, metallic

gold. A lovely display for those special keepsake ornaments, it can be used year after year.

Ribbons, greens, and antique ornaments glued to a sphere (above) create a contemporary ornament. A red organza ribbon, gold metallic leaf, and a silk tassel (below) turn this ordinary pine cone into a special keepsake ornament.

A cone turned upside down (above) becomes a custom-made ornament with a tartan ribbon hanger. Styrofoam® balls (below) can be covered with dried rosemary, nutmeg, or dill seed for a culinary accent.

Golden cords help this modern Santa (right) tote his bag so generously filled with a bundle of beautiful stems of lavender, permanent grapes, and a blossom of permanent hydrangea. This Santa brings charm to any room. Small, brick-red garden pots (below) showcase wood chip covered spheres. Available in different sizes, the premade ornaments can be stacked. Or, to create a traditional topiary, one ball can be placed on a stick. Red berries and green holly leaves add bright accents.

An oversized, plastic ornament (opposite page) forms an unusual but festive container for this holiday design. The hanger hole of the ornament is used as the vase's mouth. To create the base, hot-glue the center of a roll of floral tape to the bottom of the ornament. Reminiscent of an old-fashioned gazing ball, this frosted purple ornament (below) becomes the central focus in this vase of permanent hydrangeas, grapes, stems of lavender, and ivy leaves. A bow fashioned out of gold mesh ribbon and maroon and gold ribbon adds a complementary accent to the varying shades of purple in the design.

An ornate, jewel-encrusted heart (left) and gilded foliage give this prettily wrapped package a quaint Victorian style.

Candles

Representing the joy and hope of Christmas, candles bring a bright warmth and cozy glow into every home.

Simple yet dramatic red tapers of varying heights (above) add charm and elegance and evoke a holiday mood.

A mound of dried pepper-berries (above) and plumosa fern provide a base for this candle.

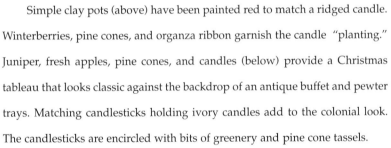

Simple clay pots (above) have been painted red to match a ridged candle. Winterberries, pine cones, and organza ribbon garnish the candle "planting." Juniper, fresh apples, pine cones, and candles (below) provide a Christmas tableau that looks classic against the backdrop of an antique buffet and pewter trays. Matching candlesticks holding ivory candles add to the colonial look. The candlesticks are encircled with bits of greenery and pine cone tassels.

This urn (above) overflows with red canella berries which surround a banded pillar candle.

The glow of Gothic candles (above) lights up this angel that is customized with swirls of pepperberry and parchment hydrangea blooms. The candles rest in small birds' nests. One nest is trimmed with tiny pine cones and cranberry red ribbon, and the other nest is adorned with a sheaf of lavender and a rose. In this glittery centerpiece (left), the metallic gold candle has been dropped into a glass cylinder vase. The vase assures safety while adding extra shine to the composition. Some of the ornaments remain their original metallic tone, while others are marbelized for a cosmopolitan mix. Dried statice adds a rich, warm contrast to the reflective sheen.

This column of pepperberries (below) has the allure of a medieval laurel wreath. Pine cones, dianthus, and agapanthus florets add to the style.

Dramatically heralding the approach of the holidays, this regal trio of candles (above) features teal, purple, and gold. Ceramic containers adorned with gold lamé leaves, permanent violets, and blackberries also display the deep jewel tones.

These candle treats (above) herald an English tea party. When burned, they create the scents of spiced apple, plum pudding, and butter rum balls. Permanent fruits and greens add antique style.

A masculine Christmas look (above) is achieved by converting a metal urn, a bronze vase, and a basket covered with moss and twigs into candle holders. Magnolias, pears, and a trio of alstroemeria blossoms lend haven to a partridge. This design (left) is created by binding moss, tallowberry, and eucalyptus to the side of a glass cylinder with wire. A candle is placed in the inverted cylinder, and a matching ribbon is glued at the base. This spicy candle treatment (right) is created by trimming cinnamon sticks to the right height and binding them in place with a hidden rubber band. A pine cone rosette garnishes the bow.

This pheasant-feathered fantasy (left) features a ball-shaped candle placed atop a candlestick commonly used for a tall taper. Pheasant plumes serve as a visual connector between the arrangement's two focal points, one at the base of the design and the other at the top. Mosses, bits of ribbon, berries, pine cones, and metallic gold ornaments accent the focal areas. The gleam of the ornament-shaped candle beautifully offsets the hues of the hawthorn berries. The Christmas colors adorning the flickering candle lend a holiday glow to any room.

A brass bowl (below) is filled with green apples, white snapdragons, red gerberas, and mini carnations. Stacked-apple candlesholders support glowing hurricane lamps topped off with bows of festively striped ribbon. To create an apple candlestick, hot-glue a plastic extender rod to a foam board base. Core three apples and thread them onto the extender rod. Glue a plastic candleholder pick, with the spike removed, to the top of the extender rod, and adhere the hurricane lamp to the top. The candlesticks and the brass bowl centerpiece add colonial style to any table, but they evoke the era of colonial Williamsburg particularly well when showcased with antique pewter trays and pitchers.

Peppermint-patterned candles (above), real candy, and a candle wrapped in cellophane create a festive mood. The bases of these distinctive candles (left) are glass vases filled with colored water. Red, white, and green ribbon adds holiday sparkle. A bubble bowl (right) is given peppermint pizzazz by squirting red, white, and green acrylic paint inside the bowl, allowing each application to dry thoroughly.

CANDLE HINTS

VOTIVES

• Use votive candles to create pools of light around a table. Add a tablespoon of water to the bottom of the votive cup to help with clean-up and extinguish the candle if it burns down.

• Votive candles used on a table exaggerate the lines in people's faces. Add a flattering glow with 24-, 30-, or 36-inch tapers to melt away years.

TAPERS

• When using taller candles of varied heights, the combination of 18-, 24-, and 10-inch candles is especially effective. Always place four to six inches apart. A 36-inch taper looks best alone.

• Tall candles with a half-inch diameter are economical, but they won't fit a standard candelabrum. However, inserting them directly into the floral foam works quite effectively.

• Trim the base, rather than the top, from a candle that is too tall.

ARRANGING

• Candles of the same height, width, and brand burn down evenly. Use three or five candles of the same height to create a dramatic effect.

• Vary diameters and colors of candles in arrangements for a sense of opulence. Assorted candles will burn at different speeds. Use matching candleholders for a unifying effect.

BURNING TIPS

• When estimating burn times for candles, reduce suggested time by 30 percent to accommodate drafts. Candles burn faster and drip more when they are in line with ventilation drafts.

• Thinner candles handle drafts better.

• If a candle starts smoking, extinguish it and shorten the wick. Do not relight until the wax has solidified.

• To avoid self-smothering, burn columns for three to four hour periods.

CANDLEHOLDERS

• Floral tape wrapped around a candle's base will keep the candle stable.

• Spray a candelabrum with cooking oil to discourage wax buildup.

STORAGE

• If a candle is stored in foam overnight or longer, place foil over the end to keep the wick from absorbing moisture.

• Always store candles in their original box and avoid laying them crisscross.

• Storing candles in the refrigerator may help them to burn longer. Sunlight or fluorescent light fades candles faster than incandescent light.

• To make candles appear new, shape the tip with a candle resharper and use again.

LIGHTING & EXTINGUISHING

• Trim new candle wicks to half an inch before burning it for the first time.

• Remove black lumps of carbon from a wick before lighting. If the carbon ignites, the candle will burn unevenly.

• Butane fireplace lighters are good for lighting candles, especially at weddings, when there are several.

• A good way to snuff out a candle is to bend the wick into the liquid wax.

Christmas
Elements

Holiday Greens

Greens are one of the most important design elements in holiday arrangements. Many varieties are fragrant, long lasting, and available throughout the winter months. Proper care and handling can help greens stay fresh longer; most need frequent watering, regular misting, and cool temperatures.

BALSAM

BLOOMED INCENSE

DOUGLAS FIR

HEMLOCK

INCENSE CEDAR

BERRIED JUNIPER

NOBLE FIR

PONDEROSA PINE

PRINCESS PINE

PORT ORFORD

RED CEDAR

SCOTCH PINE

SILVER TIPPED FIR

WHITE FIR

Holly

Holly has long been a holiday tradition, not only as a favorite element in seasonal decorations, but also as a universal symbol for Christmas itself. Everyone loves berry-laden holly for the cheer it provides in its presentation of Christmas colors. During the Victorian era, holly was symbolic of domestic happiness and foresight, according to the language of flowers. Today, holly adds a festive feeling to mantels and doorways. Its versatility as a cherished Christmas foliage is timeless.

LEGENDS

Holly has been a part of medicines and magic, science and superstitions, and legend and lore since the time of the Greeks, the Romans, and the Druids. Several countries and cultures have held particular beliefs about holly.

ITALY: In parts of Italy, sprigs of holly were used in decorating mangers in commemoration of the Infant Savior.

GERMANY: In Germany, holly is called Christdorn—the thorn woven into the crown of crucifixion. Legend has it that the berries of holly were once yellow, but being stained from the wounds of Christ, have remained red ever since.

PENNSYLVANIA DUTCH: To the older generations of the Pennsylvania Dutch, the holly berries represented the blood of Christ and the white flowers of the holly tree were symbolic of the purity in which He was conceived.

ENGLAND: In London, in 1598, the parish churches, street corners, and marketplaces, as well as every house, were decorated with holly at Christmas. It was estimated that in 1851, in London, 250,000 bunches were sold. In parts of England, it was considered decidedly unlucky to leave holly up after New Year's Eve, or Twelfth Night, lest the maidens of the household be visited by a ghost for each leaf in the decorations.

WALES: In Wales, if holly was brought indoors before Christmas Eve, it was sure to cause family quarrels throughout the year.

ULSTER SCOTS OF PENNSYLVANIA: In Pennsylvania, if holly was brought into the house during good weather, the wife would master the household for the ensuing year; if it was brought inside during rough weather, the husband would be the ruler.

INDIANS OF EARLY PENNSYLVANIA: These Indians regarded holly as their "Red Badge of Courage" and the token of success in battle. They used preserved berries as decorative buttons on their vests and sleeves, and in their hair.

CARE & HANDLING

When fresh holly is purchased in bunches, it should be recut under water and placed in a preservative solution. Since holly is one of the less hardy Christmas greens, it is very sensitive to ethylene gas. One of the most common producers of ethylene is fresh fruit, so avoid placing holly arrangements near bowls of fruit.

Arrangements featuring holly will last for one to two weeks. Do not mist holly, since spotting or molding may occur as a result. Frequent watering of holly is important. And, remember not to place holly arrangements on fireplace mantels and radiators or near heat vents.

DECORATING WITH HOLLY

Holly can be used in a variety of ways to decorate homes for the Christmas season. Holly wreaths, perfect for welcoming visitors, can grace windows and doors, while sprigs of holly tucked into banister garlands also provide a festive Christmas look. Try gluing sprigs of fresh holly into the loops of gift package bows for a fresh gift wrapping idea.

Pine Cones

Pine cones are key elements in holiday arrangements. They provide an inexpensive way to bring a touch of nature indoors while evoking a sense of colonial America. Today there are over 100 known varieties of pine cones gathered in countries all over the world. This section showcases the versatility of pine cones.

ADLER

ASTRICA

BLEACHED ASTRICA

GIANT SEQUOIA

LARCH

LODGEPOLE

PINION

PONDEROSA

PRINCESS

SCOTCH

SPRUCE

WHITE PINE

WHITE SPRUCE

Popular Pine Cones

Pine cones are more than just pretty accessories. They can also be used to create unique candleholders and to cover containers in stunning fashion. Clumps of moss complete the woodland motif and add softness.

This pine cone wreath (left) harbors a collection of pears, canella berries, nuts, and pomegranates. Having traditional holiday colors replaced with subtle earth tones, this wreath transcends the season from Thanksgiving through the new year.

An exquisite pine cone wreath (right), complete with canella berries, curling pheasant feathers, permanent holly, and preserved magnolia leaves, hangs from a length of traditional tartan ribbon. The cluster at the top of the swag is made of a permanent poinsettia attached to a bow of the same ribbon. A vertical arrangement, such as this one, can easily decorate many areas; it can be hung on a door, above a fireplace mantel, or on a window frame.

This unique topiary (left), highlighted by a lacquered rose among the pine cones, includes traditional holly, wintergreens, and tartan ribbon—always treasured favorites. The top is supported with an addition of cones and permanent leaves and berries hot-glued around the rose. The ribbon forms a connecting visual element between the topiary ball and the terra-cotta container.

Christmas Trees

Over 36 million American families celebrate the holidays with a real Christmas tree. And many of them have a favorite species. Some prefer the same type of tree they had when growing up. For others, tree preference has more to do with the color, needle length, shape, fullness, fragrance, and lasting quality.

The top-selling species in the U.S. are Douglas fir, Scotch pine, Noble fir, and Fraser fir. Growers note that sales of Douglas fir and Scotch pine are declining and that Fraser fir is rapidly gaining popularity in all areas of the country. Firs are generally the longest lasting cut trees for the holidays.

The life of a fresh evergreen tree can be extended by taking a few simple steps. Cut the trunk off a least half an inch above the original cut. If the tree is not taken inside after the fresh cut has been made, it should be stored in a shaded place with the stump placed in a bucket of water. Once the tree is brought inside, it should be placed in a stand that holds at least one gallon of water. An average tree will "drink" between one quart and one gallon of water every day. Check the tree's water level daily and do not let it drop below the cut end.

Fraser Fir

Needles are soft, flat, and short, 3/8" - 1 1/4". They are rounded at the tip, with a broad, circular base. The color is dark green with a silvery underside. Very good needle retention.

Douglas Fir

Horizontal branches with pendulous branchlets. Needles are flat and short, 3/4" - 1 1/4". The color ranges from dark yellow green to bright green to bluish-green. Needles are spread in two rows.

Balsam Fir

Needles are flat and short, 4/5" - 1 1/2", and are rounded at the tip. They are singly attached and form a very soft, feather-like spray of foliage. They are very fragrant and have strong boughs.

Scotch Pine

Needles are long, 1 1/2" - 3", usually twisted, stiff, and flattened, occurring in clusters of two. The color is grayish-green to bright, dark green to bluish-green.

White Pine

Branches are dense and horizontal. Needles are long, 2"- 5", and are soft, flexible, slender, and occur in clusters of five. The branches are a bluish-green, with moderately strong boughs.

Colorado Blue Spruce

Needles are short, about 1" long, and are prickly and sharp. They are singly attached on all sides around the twigs. The color of the branches is silvery-gray to bluish-green.

A FLORISTS' REVIEW ENTERPRISES, INC. BOOK

©1996, FLORISTS' REVIEW ENTERPRISES, INC.
ALL RIGHTS RESERVED. PUBLISHED 1996

FLORISTS' REVIEW CHRISTMAS WAS DESIGNED AND PRODUCED BY
FLORISTS' REVIEW ENTERPRISES, INC.
3641 SW PLASS TOPEKA, KS 66604-0368

ISBN 0-9654149-0-6

PRINTED IN THE UNITED STATES BY THE JOHN HENRY COMPANY, LANSING, MI
SEPARATIONS & POSTSCRIPT SERVICES BY CAPITAL GRAPHICS, INC., TOPEKA, KS

THE TEXT OF THIS BOOK WAS EXCERPTED OR ADAPTED FROM ARTICLES PUBLISHED IN
FLORISTS' REVIEW (VOL. 182, NO.7 – VOL.187, NO. 7, 1990-1996)

THE PHOTOGRAPHS IN THIS BOOK WERE PREVIOUSLY PUBLISHED IN
FLORISTS' REVIEW (VOL. 182, NO.7 – VOL.187, NO. 7, 1990-1996)